The Pioneers Go West

During the spring of 1844, eleven covered
wagons headed westward from Council Bluffs,
Iowa. Some fifty men, women, and children
with their dogs and oxen and a herd of almost
a hundred cattle made up the caravan that
plodded slowly toward California.

Within this little group of pioneers was a
spirited seventeen-year-old boy named Mose
Schallenberger, who kept a fascinating journal
of the trip. From Mose's notes George Stewart
has drawn firsthand information about the
events of that journey, from encounters with
Indians and buffalo to near-starvation and
disaster. Here is the story of these brave pioneers who miraculously succeeded in bringing
the first covered wagons to California.

The Pioneers Go West

George R. Stewart

Previously published as
To California by Covered Wagon

Random House New York

Copyright 1954 by George R. Stewart. Copyright renewed 1982
by Theodosia B. Stewart. All rights reserved under International
and Pan-American Copyright Conventions. Published in the
United States by Random House, Inc., New York, and simultaneously
in Canada by Random House of Canada Limited, Toronto.
Originally published as *To California by Covered Wagon*.

Library of Congress Cataloging-in-Publication Data:

Stewart, George Rippey.
The pioneers go west.
(Landmark books)
Rev. ed. of: To California by covered wagon. c1954.
SUMMARY: Relates the hardships encountered by a group of pioneers trav-
eling by covered wagon from Iowa to California in 1844. 1. Overland jour-
neys to the Pacific—Juvenile literature. 2. West (U.S.)—Description and
travel—To 1848—Juvenile literature. 3. Frontier and pioneer life—West
(U.S.)—Juvenile literature. [1. Overland journeys to the Pacific. 2. West
(U.S.)—Description and travel—To 1848. 3. Frontier and pioneer life] I.
Stewart, George Rippey. To California by covered wagon. II. Title.
F592.S798 1987 978′.02 87-4568
ISBN: 0-394-89180-5 (trade); 0-394-90342-0 (lib. bdg.)

Manufactured in the United States of America
1 2 3 4 5 6 7 8 9 0

Contents

Foreword

About 1885, when he was nearly sixty years old, Moses Schallenberger set down the story of the trip that he made to California more than forty years before. The original manuscript has disappeared, probably burned in a fire that destroyed the Schallenberger house in San Jose, California. Before that time, however, it had been in the hands of Horace S. Foote, and he had reproduced most of it in his history of San Jose called *Pen Pictures. The Pioneers Go West,* even in its details, is primarily based upon the story as preserved by Foote. I have been able to add certain details from the reminiscences of other members of the Stevens party and from my own knowledge of the country.

The Foote version is exactly reproduced in a volume which I have edited under the title *The Opening of the California Trail* and which has been published by the University of California Press.

GEORGE R. STEWART

The Pioneers Go West

1 _____

Mose Starts
for California

It was the spring of 1844. At that time the
United States did not include California. Just
the same, many Americans wanted to go
there. They had heard fabulous stories, even
then, of its fine climate and rich lands. But
California was far away and frighteningly
difficult to reach. From the westernmost
farms in Missouri it was at least two thousand miles and of course there was no railroad. There was not even a road for wagons.

Yet some pioneers had already struggled

across to Oregon in covered wagons. That was some help because emigrants to California could follow the Oregon Trail for about halfway. Beyond that point, however, everything was uncertain. Two parties had actually tried to go through to California with wagons, and neither of them had made it. They had abandoned their wagons in the desert and had to grope their way ahead on horseback or afoot. The only choice was between pushing on and dying.

It is natural to ask why people who wanted to go to California did not ride all the way on horseback. That was possible and would have been a relatively safe way of getting there if you were a young man wanting to make the journey all by yourself. But many of the people who were setting out for California were men with wives and children. Besides, there was no point going all the way to California

4

if you had to arrive there empty-handed and poor. The very least a group of pioneers could bring with them would be quilts and blankets, pots and pans, and, most important of all, farming tools. In addition it would be wise to carry as many things as possible to sell at a high profit to the rich Mexican cattle ranchers in California. With this money one could buy land of one's own and get a start at farming.

Before that May of 1844 no one had ever driven wagons clear across to California. It was not unusual that Elisha Stevens should want to try. For many years he had been a trapper on the headwaters of the Missouri, and he knew the plains and the mountains. He had heard, as every frontiersman had, of the wonders of faraway California. But he also knew from his own experience, and from all the tales told in camp and outpost of the

5

hazards of the journey through the un-
tracked wilderness.

Hawk-nosed, long-headed Elisha Stevens
was a stickler for organization, and he had to
be. In the group he gathered around him
were twenty-six men—if we count among the
men two seventeen-year-old boys, Moses
Schallenberger and his friend John Murphy.
There were also eight women and sixteen
children, boys and girls, some of them only
babies.

The oldest of them all was Greenwood, a
trapper, who claimed to be eighty years old.
At once "Old Greenwood" was hired as offi-
cial guide because he knew most about the
land they would have to cover. At least he
could lead the way until they had to leave the
Oregon Trail.

Then there was Dr. Townsend, a real doctor, who like many physicians in those days

6

was a good farmer, too. His farm in Missouri was near the town of St. Joseph, at the western edge of the state that was close to the Missouri River, in real backwoods country. Just across the river—what is now Kansas—was Indian country. Dr. Townsend was married to Mose Schallenberger's older sister.

A third old trapper was named Hitchcock. His daughter and grandchildren were traveling with him. Like Greenwood, he knew a great deal about the trail.

There was a Canadian by the name of Dennis Martin. There were also many Irish people, with good Irish names like Sullivan and Murphy.

And if we are to have a hero it may as well be Mose Schallenberger because Mose lived through the most amazing adventures on the whole journey. Besides, he wrote down what happened, and we have his record to rely on.

His is a true story and we can believe it, even in the little things—about how he crawled past the buffalo's nose, for instance, and how he lost his pistols.

The only picture we have of Mose is one that was taken many years later. Then he was a grown man and had a fine black beard reaching clear down to the first button on his vest. Even from this picture, we can judge that he was a handsome boy, with a firm mouth and a strong sharp nose, with heavy eyebrows and dark piercing eyes that seemed to be on the lookout for a distant buffalo or Indian. Although the picture shows only his head and shoulders, the way he holds himself makes us believe him to have been tall and strong.

Mose's father had come from Switzerland, and his mother from Germany. He was born in Ohio, the youngest of a big family. His parents died when he was six years old. After that he lived with his sister, Mrs. Townsend. At first they lived in Pennsylvania and then in Indiana and then in Ohio again. But for the last two years their home had been in Missouri.

As a boy Mose learned what a backwoods boy was likely to learn. He knew how to drive oxen and how to ride horseback. He was a fine shot with a rifle and liked to hunt. Also— and this is worth remembering because it is important in the story—Mose knew something about trapping. Because Missouri has mild winters and not very heavy snows, Mose knew nothing about snowshoes—and this also is something to remember.

For a while he went to a log schoolhouse, where he learned to read and write. He liked to read books, but even more than reading he liked to play pranks. His high spirits made him reckless, and he could lose his temper and get fighting mad.

This is the kind of boy Mose was. But why was he going to California? First of all, of course, he was going because his sister and Dr. Townsend were going. They were like his own father and mother to him, and he wanted to be with them. The Townsends were going because Mrs. Townsend was not well, and the doctor had heard that the California climate was good for sick people. But Dr. Townsend also had ideas about getting rich, so he kept moving from place to place. For different reasons, both Dr. Townsend and Mose must have been greatly excited to be going out into a strange country that was called the West.

The entire Stevens party traveled in eleven wagons. These were of the kind that people sometimes call prairie schooners, but in those early days they were called just covered wagons. Actually they were nothing at all except ordinary farm wagons such as any farmer had in those times. They became covered wagons when you changed them into a moving tent by putting an arched canvas cover over them. This cover was held in place by long thin strips of hickory wood, about as big around as a man's finger and bent into loops.

The wagons were pulled by oxen, yoked in teams of two. A wagon usually needed two or three teams. Oxen are better for this kind of journey than horses. To be sure, horses walk faster and pull a wagon much farther in one day. To make a journey of a week, or of a month even, horses are better. But for a journey of five or six months, oxen are what you want. They can endure more hardship and can live better on grass than horses can.

In addition to the team oxen the Stevens party had other oxen for spares and to be used for food if necessary. So altogether they must have started out with a herd of almost a hundred cattle.

The men and boys, and some of the women, too, had riding horses. Such horses could go through to California well enough because they would not be worked as hard as if they were pulling wagons.

Mose does not mention any dogs, but we can be sure that there were some. Dogs were useful to help herding the stock, to give alarms about Indians at night, and sometimes for hunting. But most of all we can be sure that there were dogs because wherever people go they like to take their dogs along.

Possibly a few women even brought their cats. We can be pretty certain, however, that there were no sheep or pigs or chickens. The long trip would have been very hard on them. There was no use taking them anyway, for there were plenty of such animals in California.

On the evening of May 15, 1844, the Stevens party was encamped at Council Bluffs, where now stands the city of that name, in Iowa. This was the jumping-off place. It was the farthest outpost of the frontier. Beyond, to the west, everything was Indian country.

The camp was on the bank of the broad and muddy Missouri River. Anyone standing there in the camp and looking toward the west would think first, that evening, of the river. To cross it with all those oxen and wagons was the first test. But beyond that, even more frightening, lay the long haul to California. There was no place to stop halfway. There was no place where they could make a winter camp. And at the farther end, just before they came down into the rich valley of California, the highest mountains of all rose up like a jagged-topped wall. On them the snow lay deep in the winter. They must cross those mountains before the snow fell, or they might never cross them at all.

The mountains and deserts were far away and would have to wait for a while. Close at hand, the wide brown river that people called the Big Muddy gurgled and swirled on through the darkness. The first thing the Stevens party had to do, next day, was to get across that river.

2 _____

Across
the Missouri

In the morning the sun was at their backs as they looked out across the river. It was broad, and the green shore that was the Indian country looked far off.

First of all, they set about getting the wagons across. Some Oregon emigrants were wanting to cross also, and altogether there were about forty wagons. There was one little flatboat for a ferry, big enough for only one wagon at a time! When the first wagon was run on board, it stood up high and almost seemed to overbalance the boat. But it got across all right.

Then the boat came back empty, and another wagon was loaded on. Thus it went—steady work, but slow.

Also they had to get the animals across. With so many wagons, there was a herd of several hundred oxen. To try to take all these across in the little flatboat would have meant several days' work. So the men decided to make the oxen swim.

This was easy to say. But how do you do it? When the oxen were driven down to the edge of the swiftly running water, they snorted and tossed their horns and balked. The men on horseback pressed in behind, shouting and cracking whips, and at last forced the oxen to take to the water and swim. Everything looked fine.

Then trouble started. Oxen naturally follow a leader. Soon a strong ox was swimming ahead, and the others were trailing after him. But this first ox, being low down in the water, probably could not see the western shore at all. To him it must have looked as if he were swimming right out into the ocean. He did not like this, and so he started to swim back to the side of the river that he had just left.

He could not turn right around because the others were behind him. So he turned downstream and began to swim back in a loop, the others still following. But when he got near the bank, the men on horseback cracked their whips and shouted. He swerved and then saw some oxen swimming ahead of him, and made for them—happy to have something to follow.

But these oxen were the tail end of the line already following the first one. So you can see what had happened. The whole herd had formed a big circle. Each ox was swimming after the one in front of him. The whole circle of swimming cattle was just revolving—not getting toward the other side at all!

But it was even worse than that. The swift current was taking the herd downstream. Besides, the cattle were getting tired. They were frightened, and each began trying to get out of the water by climbing up on the back of the one in front. It looked suddenly as if the cattle might be swept away and drowned, and the whole journey wrecked before it was even started.

The men quickly realized that something must be done, and so they stopped urging the cattle away from the bank. The herd came ashore then, but unfortunately at a very muddy place. Many of the cattle got stuck in the mud. The men had to go in with picks and spades and dig around until the poor animals could get free. A few were so deeply stuck that they could not be got out at all, but had to be left to drown or to smother in the mud.

It had almost been a disaster at the very beginning, and for a while no one could think of anything to do. Then someone had a new idea, and this was tried out.

They picked out one of the gentlest of the oxen and tied a rope around its horns. Two men in a canoe took the other end of this rope and paddled out into the river with it. Other men cracked their whips behind. In a little while the ox was in deep water and had to swim. Then the men in the canoe could pull on the rope hard enough to keep the ox headed for the opposite shore.

Now the whole herd was again driven into the water. Again the cattle swam out after the first one, and this one was kept headed across by the men in the canoe. In a minute the river seemed half full of cattle. Now there was not a circle of frightened animals. Instead, they were all swimming steadily in the proper direction.

First was the canoe with the two men, paddling. Then came the ox with the rope around its horns, swimming. Behind came a great wedge-shaped mass of cattle—the strongest and biggest ones at the front, then the middle-sized ones, and at the rear the worried cows with their big-eyed calves swimming along beside them.

But the river was not too wide for the cattle to swim, and soon they began wading out on the other side. Even the calves made it.

By now, what with all the work of ferrying the wagons and getting the cattle to swim, it was drawing toward evening. Most of the wagons and people were still on the eastern side of the river, but a few people, along with all the cattle, had crossed to the western side. Among those few were Mose Schallenberger and his friend John Murphy.

Mose does not tell how he crossed the river. Most likely he crossed either by swimming with his horse, or else in the flatboat, holding the reins and making the horse swim behind. However it was, he was at last in the Indian country and right away that raised some problems.

This was the land of the Otoes. They were a small tribe and peaceable, but they liked to steal cattle. Now that the oxen had been safely got across the river, no one wanted to lose any of them in the night. A guard must be posted.

Captain Stevens appointed the two boys as corporals of the guard. Undoubtedly this made them both feel very grown-up and responsible, and that was probably just what the captain had in mind. He was a wise man and must have realized that the boys might get into trouble if they were not kept busy.

Ever since the cattle had arrived on the western bank, they had been allowed to graze under the guard of a herdsman. Now preparations were made for the night. First, all the wagons that had crossed were arranged in a circle. The tongue of each wagon was placed on a hind wheel of the one in front of it. Thus a kind of fort was formed. Then the cattle were driven up and attached to the wagons by chains. Finally a guard was set, just as in a camp of soldiers. Each man had to stand guard for two hours, and then a relief was marched around and new sentries posted. Each relief was under the command of a corporal of the guard. And the

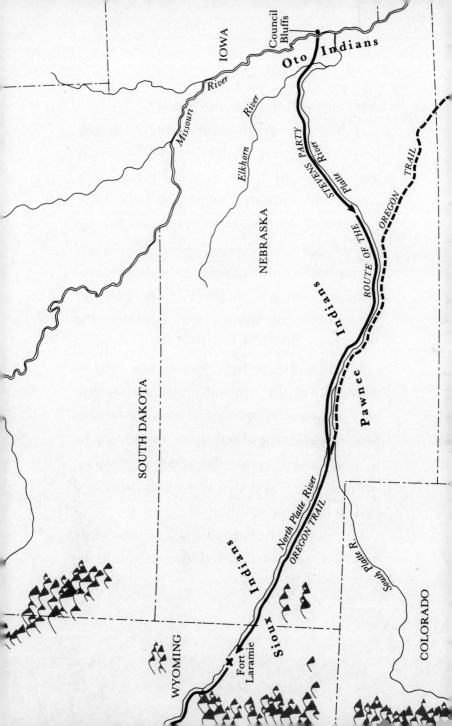

two corporals were Mose and John.

At first the boys felt important, but as time passed, they began to get bored. The night was quiet, and there was really very little chance of Indians being anywhere near. About midnight the two boys decided to stir up some fun.

One of the men in the company was named John Sullivan, a very clever fellow. Later he made a lot of money and founded the Hibernia Bank, which is still a large bank in California. But at first he was not used to being out in the wilds at night, and he was very nervous about Indians. Also he was probably worried about other things, for he was only twenty years old and was traveling with his sister and two young brothers and had to look out for them.

His fear of Indians gave an idea to Mose and John. They decided that it would be fun, and do no harm, to play a joke.

So John crept quietly up through the dark. He unloosened Sullivan's cattle and drove them off. Then he returned and gave the alarm. Sullivan jumped up, seized his gun, and ran off in pursuit.

After a long chase he and the others caught up with the cattle, found no Indians, and drove the cattle back to the wagons. Everything was quiet again, and Sullivan curled up in his blankets and went to sleep.

No sooner was he breathing heavily than the boys again unloosed the oxen and drove them off, even farther this time. Again they returned, crying the alarm. Now Sullivan jumped up, even more excited, shouting out what he thought of these thieves of Indians. Again he seized his gun and ran off. The oxen were clear out of sight in the darkness, but they could be followed by the sound of the chains they were dragging.

Sullivan jumped to the top of a log and stood there listening for the sound. John happened to be lying beside this log, and when he saw Sullivan above him he fired off his gun. Sullivan jumped into the air, and then raced off to the wagons, crying out that he had been shot by an Indian.

In the meantime someone else had caught up with the cattle and was driving them back. Sullivan was by this time so much alarmed that he did not even try to go to sleep, but stood guard over his cattle until daylight. All this was much fun for the boys and the other men who had been told of the joke.

Next morning Captain Stevens praised the courage and skill of the two boys who had twice brought the cattle back. He was surprised, he said, that the Indians should have picked out Sullivan's oxen both times and left all the others alone. The boys, with straight faces, explained this by pointing out that Sullivan's oxen were white, and so could be better seen in the dark.

Captain Stevens, even though he knew or guessed a good deal, was too wise a man to try to do anything further. He must have known that boys have to have their fun, and probably he was glad that the youngsters in his company were so high-spirited.

The joke must have seemed very funny at the time. Mose remembered it so well that he wrote it down in his story many years later. What helped give a point to the joke was Sullivan himself. He liked to boast, and after that night he used to make a big story of his near escape from death at the hands of the bloodthirsty Indians.

3 _____

Rolling Westward

Two days later all the wagons had been ferried across. It was the morning of May 18.

"Catch up your teams, boys! Catch up your teams!" That was the cry that was shouted through the camp. It meant that each man was to yoke his oxen and get everything ready to go. Time to be starting!

After that they got rolling. Day after day the long train of ox-pulled wagons moved slowly on into the west. All the open country was bright green with grass and speckled red

28

and blue and yellow with the first wildflowers.

There was just a trail, not really a road—only some faint wheel tracks, always winding a little. A few men on horseback rode ahead as scouts, keeping their rifles ready. Next came the long train of wagons. With all the teams and the forty wagons and the gaps between them, it must have stretched out to be a mile long.

Beside each team of oxen a man or boy was walking, now and then prodding the oxen with a long stick or cracking a whip over their backs to keep them moving. The oxen paid little attention and kept moving ahead, but so slowly that they seemed to think separately for every step they decided to take.

In the wagons rode women and little children, some looking out from under the canvases, front and back. Sometimes the women would walk to stretch themselves. The older children walked also and easily kept up with the slow oxen and even ran about from one wagon to another.

Then there were the dogs too, trotting along, perhaps beneath the wagons to get away from the heat of the sun. And also, a little toward the sides of the wagons, were some mounted men with their rifles, keeping watch.

Finally, behind the wagons came the herd of extra cattle and horses, with a few more mounted men riding herd on them.

So it went, day after day. They were going west across what is now the state of Nebraska, following close to the line of the present Highway 30 and the Union Pacific Railroad. But they were moving so slowly that to us they would hardly seem to be moving at all. Fifteen miles was a good day's journey for an ox team, a distance that a modern car can travel in less than half an hour.

The only thing that broke up this first part of the journey was the Elkhorn River. When they came to it, Mose must have wondered: "*Now* what do we do?" The Elkhorn was nowhere nearly as wide as the Missouri, but still it was so deep that the oxen would have to swim. But oxen cannot swim and pull wagons behind them. There was no ferryboat.

But you could trust old-timers like Captain Stevens to know what to do. The men took the wagon boxes off a few of the wagons, covered them with rawhides to make them waterproof, and thus had some boats. They were good-sized boats, but not nearly large enough to ferry a wagon across. Still, there was a way.

The men unloaded all the forty wagons and ferried everything across in the make-shift boats. Next they took the wagons to pieces, so that there were just a lot of wheels and axles and tongues, and sides and ends and tops. Then the men put these parts, a few at a time, into the boats and ferried them over the river. Then they sorted out the parts—all the wheels and axles and tops and everything—and put them together again. In the meantime the horses and oxen had been swum across the river, and the women and children had been brought over a few at a time in the boats. Finally, all the things that had been unloaded from the wagons on the east bank were loaded back again on the west bank.

All this took several days of hard work, but in the end it was finished, and there was the wagon train all put together again and ready to start rolling on.

When they started again, some of the people must have felt more worried than before.

Up to this point, if they had wanted to, they could merely have turned around and gone back. But now, with a river like that behind them, they could not very well go back alone.

Some of them also must have worried about coming to another deep river. They couldn't afford to stop very often and work so hard and spend so much time just to cross one stream. But fortunately, as Old Greenwood could tell them, they were coming into drier country now, and there were no more bad rivers.

Then they went on again—day after day. By now they were learning how to travel.

They had left the country of the Otoes and had come to where they could expect to meet Pawnees. A few years before, the Pawnees had been a powerful and warlike tribe. But they had met with very bad luck. Many of them had died in an outbreak of small-

33

pox. After that they had been defeated in wars with other tribes.

One day there was great excitement in the train at the news that they were just about to arrive at a Pawnee village. Mose and John must have been excited at the thought of seeing some of these famous warriors of the plains in their war paint and eagle feathers. As it turned out, this village of the Pawnees had lately suffered badly in war with the Sioux. The warriors had almost been wiped out. Only women, children, and old men were seen in the village.

The boys may have been disappointed at this, but the older men, like Dr. Townsend and Captain Stevens, must have been re-lieved. At least there was nothing to fear from the Pawnees.

A week or more later the Stevens party was in what is now western Nebraska, where

34

the boys saw their first buffaloes. It was not a real herd, but merely a few bulls so old that they were no longer able to hold their own against the young bulls and had been driven away from the herd. Wild with excitement, Mose and John galloped off on their first buffalo hunt.

They picked out one big bull, fired, and wounded him. In confusion he galloped off toward the wagons as if he were going to charge right upon the women and children. Too excited to aim well, the boys followed after, shooting and shooting. Again and again they hit the bull but could not seem to bring him down. Finally he fell only fifty feet from a wagon.

Mose and John must have been very proud until they found that they had put about twenty balls into the bull before killing him. This was nothing to be proud of, for they had wasted a lot of powder and lead. Also, when they tried to cut a juicy fresh steak out of the old bull, they found that he was so stringy and tough that the meat was scarcely fit to eat. Probably some of the older hunters laughed at the boys. Still, they had killed their first buffalo, and that was something.

Actually the old bull was a pitiful creature, but the boys had probably done a good deed by shooting him. Soon the wolves would have set upon him. They would have worried and nipped and slashed at him for days until finally they brought him down. The boys had brought him to his end much more mercifully.

Not long after this the party came to a real buffalo herd, and then there was more hunting and good fresh meat to be broiled at the campfires.

36

4 ⎯⎯⎯⎯⎯⎯⎯⎯⎯⎯⎯⎯⎯⎯⎯

Mose Loses
His Pistols

After they had been on the road for a month
and it was past the middle of June, there
began to be a new interest among the
emigrants. They were approaching Fort
Laramie. This was only a fur traders' post,
not a real fort, but it marked the end of the
first stage of the journey. Arriving there
meant that they would have traveled more
than five hundred miles.

When they came into sight of the fort at
last, even Mose and John must have felt that

they were seeing plenty of Indians. The pointed buffalo-skin tepees seemed to cover the whole country, and in the encampment were no fewer than four thousand Sioux. They were real Plains Indians, their warriors riding ponies and armed with lances and bows and arrows.

Luckily the Sioux had come into the post to trade and were not wanting to fight. A sign of this, as the white men noted with relief, was that they had their women and children along with them.

All the people in the Stevens party went into camp at Fort Laramie and stayed there for several days, letting the oxen rest and feed on the good grass. There was nothing more important than keeping the oxen in good shape. Besides, there were dozens of things to be done, now that they had been traveling for more than a month and were going to be in one place for a few days.

You can guess that the mothers got out their biggest kettles and heated water in them and washed all the clothes. Also you can be sure they gave the children baths and scrubbed them hard and washed their hair because this was probably the first good chance for hot baths since they had started.

The fathers had things to do, also, besides repacking. On every wagon a tar bucket swung from an axle. At Fort Laramie the men must have got the tar buckets out, and taken each wheel off and greased it. Also the wagons probably took some other repairing, for in the dry air of the plains the boards and spokes were likely to shrink and get loose.

Of course everyone was excited—and probably a little scared, too—at having so many Indians around. Some of the men traded a few horses for Indian ponies. There are always a few men who like to trade horses, and now they thought that the ponies might be hardier and better fitted for the mountains. Some of the emigrants also bought moccasins to replace worn-out boots.

At last one morning again came the cry, "Catch up!" Then the oxen were yoked once more, and the mile-long string of wagons moved out of camp, still pointed west.

After leaving the fort the people were nervous. There was a good chance that some of the young Sioux might make up a war party, follow along behind, and watch for a chance to steal some horses—or even take a few scalps. So a more careful watch was kept, and on the trail the wagons were well bunched for protection. After a few days, since there was no attack, the people relaxed and felt comfortable again.

During this time there had been no chance

to shoot buffalo, and everyone had grown hungry for some fresh meat. Now that there seemed to be no more reason to fear Indians, Mose and John decided to go hunting again. By this time they considered themselves old hands, and as they saddled their horses early one morning, they told everybody that they would be back with a good supply of steaks. In addition to his rifle Mose took a fine pair of pistols that he carried in a special belt. The pistols would be of no use in shooting buffalo, but he still may have thought there was a chance of meeting Indians. Or perhaps he was proud of the pistols and just wore them to show them off.

Soon the boys saw a small herd of buffalo. They got off their horses and began to sneak up. Just as they were about close enough to shoot, an old bull scented them. He snorted and tossed up his tail and dashed off—the whole herd with him.

There was nothing for the boys to do but go back to their horses, mount, and follow after the buffaloes in the hope that they would settle down. After a while, sure enough, the buffaloes stopped and began grazing as before. Again the boys left their horses and tried to get close enough. But, as had happened the other time, one of the old bulls scented them and gave the alarm.

So it went all day. Perhaps these buffaloes had been hunted too much lately by the Indians and so were wary. The boys never got a shot.

At last they saw that the sun was beginning to get low in the west. They did not want to spend a night in the open, with no company except wolves and possibly Indians. They also disliked going back to camp without any meat, especially after they had boasted in the morning. Still, there was no choice. They turned their horses' heads back toward the trail.

All day, as it happened, they had seen plenty of antelope and had been within rifle shot of them. But they had scorned antelope when they had gone out after bigger game.

On their return Mose and John rode across a perfectly level plain where fine grass was growing so tall that it brushed against the horses' sides. Here many antelope were feeding, their backs scarcely showing above the grass, their heads popping out like seals' heads above water when they came up to look around.

Antelope are strange animals. Usually they dash away at the first sight or scent of man, but sometimes they are not alarmed.

These antelope were very numerous and some of them came close, as if knowing that the hunters were out for buffalo, not for antelope. But the boys had not fired a shot all day, and their trigger fingers were getting itchy.

Finally one antelope came very close, and John cried out, joking, "Why, he's going to bite me!"

He leveled his rifle, fired, and dropped the antelope in its tracks.

Mose then said it was a shame to waste the meat, and the boys dismounted and began to make the antelope ready to carry back.

But this was their bad day. While they were working, they forgot to watch the horses, which began to stray off toward camp.

When the horses were only about a hundred yards away, Mose noticed them. Thinking that he might have to chase them a long way, he quickly took off his heavy pistol belt and dropped it on the ground.

Then he ran after the horses.

He caught them with no trouble, but he noticed that one of the blankets had slipped off and been lost. He started to look for it and called for John to come and help him.

They soon found the blanket, and then they started to go back to where they had left the antelope and the rifles, and Mose's belt and pistols. Strangely, they could not find the place. In hunting for the blanket they had lost their bearings. The grass was tall enough to cover everything, and the level plain showed no landmarks. They hunted around until dusk, feeling more and more ridiculous all the time. At last there was nothing to do but start back.

They rode glumly through the darkness. That morning they had left camp bragging of all the buffalo meat they were going to bring back. Now they were returning not only without even an antelope but also without arms and ammunition. How all the older men would laugh! Even the girls would laugh!

They tried to think of excuses, and they even tried to make up some stories to explain what had happened.

"Let's say it was Indians! Let's say a whole war party of Sioux came galloping down and stopped us and took the guns away from us. Yes, they would have scalped us, if we hadn't put on a bold face and been brave about it!"

But then they decided that they could never tell such a story well enough to fool old-timers like Greenwood and Captain Stevens.

So in the end they just told the truth and had to stand for all the fun that was made of them.

Next day they went back with a party of six men, all mounted, to a spot that they knew was not more than a quarter of a mile from where they had left their rifles. All of them rode about on horseback for several hours, for no one wanted to lose the guns. But there was the plain covered with grass all about the same height, and no one ever laid eyes on either the dead antelope or the rifles or Mose's fine pistols.

5 _____

Buffalo Country

All this time the party was following the well-traveled Oregon Trail. They had been taking things easy, trying to save the strength of their oxen rather than to make fast time. By now it was early in July, and some of the families were running short of food. So it was decided to halt for a few days, shoot some buffalo, and dry the meat. The place chosen for this halt was near Independence Rock, an upstanding crag and a landmark on the trail.

So Mose went hunting again, this time with a man named Allen Montgomery. Allen was married, but he was only five or six years older than Mose. They had come from the same place in Missouri and were good friends. Allen was a gunsmith, and in fact he had made the two pistols that Mose had lost.

Soon Allen and Mose sighted a small herd of buffalo, but again things went badly. Just as before, some old bull scented them and snorted. Then the whole herd would be off.

This happened time and again, but still the two hunters kept on. It came to be afternoon, and still they had not got a shot.

Now the herd halted again near a mound of rocks. Allen and Mose decided that they might creep up behind the rocks, and then follow a little ravine and get close enough.

As they looked over the top of the mound, they saw an old bull fast asleep!

They could see the little ravine leading toward the herd, and the bull was lying just at the edge of it. They decided to try to crawl past him. This was a dangerous enough adventure for anyone. A buffalo bull, especially when suddenly aroused, is just as likely to charge at the hunters as to run away from them.

Mose and Allen began to crawl. Now they were so close in front of the bull that they could have patted his nose with the ends of their rifles. Now they were a little past him and were hoping for success.

Then suddenly the wind must have blown their scent toward the bull's nose. He jumped up, snorted, and raced off toward the herd.

Allen was so disgusted that he leveled his rifle and fired. The bull tumbled to the ground, but at the sound of the shot the herd galloped off.

Allen and Mose kept on following this herd until nearly dark. Then at last by crawling on their stomachs and hiding behind some little bushes, they managed to get to a bush about two hundred yards from the buffaloes. This was very long range for their rifles, but it was the last chance, and they decided to fire. They were both good shots, but to make sure they picked out one particular buffalo cow and both aimed at her.

"Fire!"

Each hunter pulled the trigger, the rifles cracked together, the buffalo slumped down wounded.

The hunters stayed in hiding behind the bush and reloaded. The other buffaloes, not seeing any men and not realizing what had happened, gathered around the wounded one, sniffing and pawing and bellowing. All this kept them too busy to notice anything

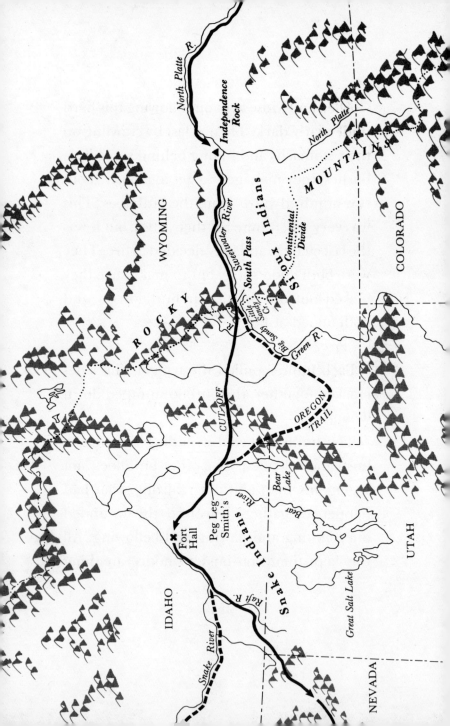

else. The hunters advanced boldly to easy rifle shot and fired again. Two more buffaloes went down, but still the herd did not take flight. Allen and Mose fired again and again. They killed seven buffaloes. Then the herd finally dashed off except for one bull. He showed fight and was about to charge when both of them fired and brought him down.

When they looked at the first buffalo they had shot they found that both bullets had struck not two inches apart. This looked like marvelous shooting until they remembered that they had aimed at the buffalo's heart and the bullets had struck three feet farther back.

The two of them had now made certain of a good supply of meat. But they still had a problem, for by now darkness had fallen and they were far from camp. The only thing to do was to sleep where they were and protect the meat—some of it, at least—from the wolves. They knew that wolves always followed a herd of buffalo, killing calves and old bulls, pulling down any buffalo that was wounded or sick, and feeding on the bodies of any that died.

Expecting that they would soon have such visitors, the two hunters picked out a spot between the bodies of two buffaloes. This was not much protection, but it was a little better than nothing. Then in the darkness they hurriedly cut out the best parts of the other buffalo and carried them to this place.

Sure enough, the wolves soon began to arrive—more and more of them. Allen and Mose were not greatly alarmed, because wolves would seldom attack a man. Besides, there was plenty of buffalo meat for them.

But the wolves were very unpleasant neighbors. They snarled and howled over the dead buffaloes so loudly that neither Allen nor Mose could sleep at all, even if anyone had wanted to sleep so close to so many wolves.

Toward morning the commotion grew even worse than before. Now instead of howling it was snapping and growling. Suddenly Allen and Mose realized that these were not all wolf growls. A bear must have arrived to get his share of meat. A grizzly!

Yes, it must be a grizzly. Only a big fellow would dare to come in and drive off so many wolves.

Now there was real cause for alarm. A single grizzly was much more dangerous than any number of wolves. Fortunately it was now near morning, and once they could see to shoot, they would no longer be defenseless.

When it was actually light, the two of them jumped up, eager to kill a grizzly, and ready to take their chances if they should only wound it.

But the bear was not so brave as some of his kind. Taking flight, he dashed off so fast that they could not get a shot.

With daylight the wolves also had drawn off, but the hunters' troubles were not yet over. They had trailed the buffaloes all day and lain awake during the night. Now, first of all, they had to build a fire and cook some buffalo meat for breakfast. Then they had to begin cutting up the buffaloes that the wolves and the bear had not eaten. This was slow and hard work. The whole morning passed. They knocked off for lunch and then went to work again. Finally, when they had finished and had packed the meat on their horses, it was three o'clock in the afternoon, and the sun was already well over toward the west.

Walking and leading their loaded horses, they traveled till dark but could find neither camp nor trail. The night was cloudy and very dark, but they kept moving. They became bewildered.

They were now in a very much more dangerous position than being close to a grizzly. Being lost is never a joke. It is especially serious in country that is not inhabited, or—even worse—may be inhabited by Indian war parties.

They stumbled on through the darkness, becoming more and more tired. Then at daybreak their luck changed, and they came suddenly to the trail. Soon they found that their luck had been doubly good, for they saw the wagons only a quarter-mile off. They came dragging their feet into camp, wholly worn out, but Mose was a great deal happier than he had been that other time when he and John Murphy returned from hunting without either meat or rifles.

The party remained a week at this camp near Independence Rock, sending out hunting parties and curing the meat that the hunters brought in. One family must have been particularly glad of this halt, for here a daughter was born to the Millers. Her parents named her Ellen Independence from the place where she was born.

After the party left Independence Rock, the next bit of excitement was the crossing of the Continental Divide, that is, the summit of the Rocky Mountains. It did not mean any steep climbing. At this point, which is called South Pass, there is a broad gap in the mountains with an easy slope on both sides. In fact, the top is so level that Mose and the others could scarcely tell when they crossed from the Atlantic to the Pacific side. Still the top of the pass is a mile and a half above the sea. Even though they could not tell because of any steep climbing that they were so high, they could tell it from the very cold nights. Also, not very far away, they could now see mountains with snow on them even in mid-summer.

Mose tells us that when they came to the first water that ran toward the Pacific, they were all happy "as though already in sight of the promised land."

6

The Cutoff— and Indians!

"Already in sight of the promised land!" Well, that was a nice idea! Some of the people, Mose tells us, now thought that they must be quite close to California. They argued that they had come a good many hundreds of miles already, so it couldn't be much farther.

Naturally it must have been only the most foolish ones who could have thought that. Anyone who had ever looked at a map would have known better. Any of the old mountain men—Captain Stevens or Hitchcock or

Greenwood—could have told them so too. In fact, they had not yet come even half the way, and they had had very good luck—no trouble with Indians, no real mishaps of any kind. The trip so far had been a good deal like a big picnic.

So far they had traveled where there was always grass and the cattle had plenty to eat. It had been buffalo country, too, where the hunters brought in plenty of fresh meat. Besides, this country was well known, and the trail was well-worn and easy to follow.

But farther to the west they would find things very different. There the country was very dry, sometimes a desert, with few streams or springs. Since there was little water, there was also little grass. There were no buffaloes, and in most places there was scarcely enough game of any kind to make hunting worthwhile. Perhaps the emigrants

might think that they had left the Sioux behind and had thus escaped from the worst of
the risks with Indians. But actually, west of
the mountains, they were likely to meet, not
Indians who were camped with their families, but war parties.

In any case, they kept on traveling. Now
for the first time since they had started, they
were following the flow of the water, not going against it. As they traveled, old man
Hitchcock began to talk about a new idea.
Like Captain Stevens and Greenwood,
Hitchcock had been in the mountains before,
and he seems to have known this particular
part of the country very well.

According to him, the first people who had
taken wagons through had gone a long way
around. First they had traveled several days'
journey too far south, and then they had
made a sharp turn and come back toward

the north. By going straight west, Hitchcock said, the party could save a hundred miles.

The party finally decided to try the cutoff, and old man Hitchcock was appointed guide for one day.

The people were so used to having an easy time of it and to being lucky that they did not send anyone on horseback to scout the road. Indeed, they didn't even carry extra water. Instead they took Hitchcock's word that the distance across from the camp on Big Sandy Creek to the next water, at Green River, was only twenty-five miles—just one long day's drive.

But they soon found that traveling without a trail was very different from traveling even on a poor trail. The country was rough and broken, and the going was very slow.

They pressed on until darkness fell and then had to halt for the night and make a camp with no water. The people were so thirsty that they could think of nothing but drinking. The cattle had worked all day at pulling the wagons, and they were even thirstier than the people. And nobody even yet knew how far it might be to the river. Old man Hitchcock must have had a lot of explaining to do.

The men set extra guards on the cattle herd that night, knowing that the thirsty animals might stampede in search of water. In spite of the guard, this actually happened, and about forty of the cattle ran off into the darkness. Luckily these were not the team oxen, but cows and calves that were driven along in the herd.

As soon as there was light to see, the men were up, yoking the oxen. They pushed on grimly—the poor oxen weak from thirst, the children frightened, the mothers trying to comfort them, the men stern-faced, and everybody thirsty. They kept plugging on steadily hour after hour as the sun got higher and grew hotter. Shortly before noon they finally came to Green River—and water.

It was good to have water, but things still looked ticklish. This was only about halfway across the cutoff, and the oxen had had a bad time of it already. Worst of all, forty cattle had been lost.

At Green River the whole party rested for the afternoon. The next morning they still stayed in camp, but Captain Stevens sent six men on horseback to hunt for the missing cattle. One of these was Mose.

The six started out together, but soon they began to argue where to go. Some thought that the cattle would have backtracked. Others thought they would have headed for some point on Green River. Not agreeing, the party split up. Mose went with those who went eastward. With him was a man named Daniel Murphy, and another named Bean.

They rode on for a long distance without seeing any cattle, and after several hours they thought that they must be halfway back across the cutoff. At this time they were riding one behind the other with Murphy in the lead.

Suddenly he ducked his head, then threw his body over the side of his horse, Indian-fashion, as if to hide. He wheeled his horse around, motioning for the others to follow. Without arguing, they did so and trailed him at full gallop up a small ravine. After a quarter of a mile Murphy pulled his horse in, and as the others came up, he said a single word: "Indians!"

The three dismounted, tied their horses, and then decided that they had better see what was happening rather than take a chance of being surprised. They crawled on their stomachs to a point where they could just look over the edge of the ravine.

Very close—far too close—they saw a party of about a hundred mounted warriors. From the feathered topknots and the general style of dress, the three men could tell that these must be Sioux. This was bad, for at that time the Sioux were considered the most dangerous of all the tribes, and this was obviously a war party. At least the three of them had been lucky to see the Indians first.

As they continued to look out cautiously, the Indians moved closer and closer. Now came the sounds of the warriors calling back and forth, talking to one another. Now the ponies were clumping by, only twenty yards away.

All the three could hope was that the Indians would keep moving. So they did, and finally the last pony disappeared over a rise. Then at last Mose and his comrades could breathe easily.

After such an experience you would have thought that they would have ridden off as fast as possible to get to the camp and give the warning. But the Indians must have been traveling north or south, and the camp lay to the west. Apparently Mose and the others thought that the people on Green River were in no danger, and that the three of them should go ahead and look for the cattle. By going east they would be getting farther away from this war party, and there was not much chance that another one would be close.

So they rode on, and near the old camp on Big Sandy Creek they found the cattle. They rounded them up, and since it was now near evening, they made camp, keeping a guard. The night passed quietly, and early in the morning they started out to drive the herd to Green River.

When they had gone only half a mile, they suddenly saw two Indians on horseback at the top of the hill about a mile distant. And this time they had not had the luck to see the Indians first. Besides, what was the chance of hiding a herd of forty cattle?

What should they do? There was no need for three men armed with rifles to be afraid of two Indians armed only with bows and arrows. The best thing to do was to push ahead boldly.

In a couple of minutes, however, they saw two more Indians in a different direction. This looked as if there were many Indians, trying to surround the white men and the cattle. Then suddenly, a few minutes later, the worst thing of all happened. Indians appeared in many directions, whooped out their war cry, and came galloping.

69

In the moment that they had to decide, Mose and the others agreed to stand firm and sell their lives dearly. Each would pick an Indian and from horseback fire a shot at close range. Then they would spur their horses, charge the Indians, and hope to break through their line and ride hard for the camp on Green River.

As the Indians came galloping close, the three held their ground, and then each threw up a hand, as a last resort, to show that they wished to talk. The Indians halted, seemed to consult, and then Mose and the others saw three warriors lay down their bows and ride forward to talk. Fifty yards away they halted and held out their hands in a sign of friendship. At that moment Mose felt a great relief, and for the first time his heart began to pound less heavily.

The Indians turned out to be a party of the Snake tribe, who were friendly to the whites. They were actually in pursuit of the band of Sioux.

The Snakes proved to be real friends. Some of them even accompanied Mose and his comrades partway toward the camp, helping to drive the cattle.

Next morning the wagon party went on across rough country, still breaking trail. It was slow going. But the second half of the cutoff turned out to be not so bad as the first, and after three or four days the Stevens party came to the traveled road again.

On the whole they had done very well by taking the cutoff. They had saved several days' travel, and in the end they had not lost any cattle. And their luck with the Indians was still holding. Also, by taking the cutoff, they had learned two useful lessons—not to think that things would always be easy and not to take risks without preparing in advance.

71

7 _____

On to California!

From the place where they came again to the Oregon Trail, ten days of traveling brought them to Fort Hall.

This was another fur traders' post, much like Fort Laramie. The party halted there for several days. By now it was the middle of August, and they had traveled more than a thousand miles, a little over halfway to California.

From here the trail led on to Oregon. But if anyone wanted to reach California, there was no use in following the Oregon Trail much farther because it ran too far to the north.

Here the ones who were going to Oregon and the ones who were going to California said their good-byes. It was sad to be parting. These people had traveled and worked together all the way from Council Bluffs and had gone through hardships and dangers together. Now they had to part without much hope that they would see one another again. For in those days the difficulty of traveling between Oregon and California was too great for anyone to think of making the trip in the ordinary course of life. Here Mose had to say good-bye to Bean, with whom he had gone to search for the cattle and had faced the charging Indians.

The Oregon party, it seems, went on first, and the California party remained at Fort

Hall a day or two longer, preparing for their even harder journey and trying to find out what lay ahead.

Yes, ahead waited the real trouble. So far they had gone across country where Greenwood and Hitchcock had already traveled. Except for the cutoff, they had followed the well-marked trail that was beaten down by the oxen and wagons of the many emigrants going to Oregon.

But neither Greenwood nor Hitchcock had traveled between Fort Hall and California, and only one party had tried it with wagons. They got through, piloted by Joe Walker— but without any wagons.

Still the people in the Stevens party would never even have started for California unless they were ready to take chances. They were for going on. They got the best directions they could and made ready to start.

During the few days' stop at Fort Hall there was all the business of washing clothes and repairing wagons, just as there had been at Fort Laramie. Food supplies were running short now except for the stores of dried buffalo meat. Some families had a little bacon left. Besides, there were the extra cattle that were being driven along and could be used for meat when necessary. But some of the people were hungry for food besides meat. At Fort Hall they were able to buy a little flour but they had to pay a dollar a pound.

Then one morning the Stevens party pushed off for California. Eleven of the big canvas-covered wagons took the trail. Walking beside the oxen, or scouting ahead, or driving the herd at the rear—altogether, they numbered twenty-six men. Some of them, like Greenwood and Hitchcock and Grandpa Murphy, were old men, and some of them, like Moses Schallenberger and John Murphy, were really boys. Still, counting them all, there were twenty-six of them to take the wagons through and stand guard and watch against Indians.

Besides the men, there were eight women, also about eight boys and eight girls.

After that, for a day or two, they still followed the Oregon Trail. Then at Raft River they turned left and struck off toward the south on the tracks of the three wagons that Joe Walker had piloted the year before.

Again they went on, day after day. The country was all valleys and rolling hills covered with sagebrush. There were mountains, but not very high mountains, and the trail either wound around the ends of them or crossed them by passes.

The trail itself did not amount to much. Three wagons with some mules and horses do not leave a very heavy mark. And after a year had passed, with rain and snow and wind, there was often almost nothing to be seen at all. In some places sand must have blown back over the wagon tracks, wiping them out. But still, if you looked ahead, you could always see—somewhere—the marks of the wagon wheels, or the broken bushes of sagebrush, or some droppings from the horses or mules.

Captain Stevens kept two or three men ahead, scouting. These men slept out, but one of them rode in with news every day. He told them what the trail was like for the next day's journey and how to go in places where it was not plain to see. Also he probably told them of places where they could save distance and make better time by taking little cutoffs or by following some easier route than the other wagon train had found. That was the way a road began—each party making it a little better.

The country was dry but it was not desert. Always at the end of the day they arrived at some spring or little stream that the scouts had found. Usually this was a place where the other party had camped also. They knew because they saw the ashes of the fires and the broken bushes where the wagon circle had stood. It was comforting to camp where the others had camped. Sometimes also they found things that the others had left behind or lost or put down and forgotten. That is why there are places named Pipe Creek and Hat Creek and Pistol Spring—because there someone found a pipe or a hat or a pistol.

After two weeks of this kind of traveling they came to a small stream flowing westward. From what they had been told at Fort Hall they must have known this to be the Humboldt River.

Here the emigrants first met some Paiute Indians. The white people called them Diggers. That was because these Indians did not ride horses or live by hunting big game, but spent much time digging for roots. They also lived on the seeds of the desert plants and on rabbits and even on lizards and rats. Old Greenwood had been able to talk to the other Indians, but he had never been among the Diggers before. He found that their language was something like that of the Snakes, and so he was able to talk a little to them by means of signs and a few of the Snake words.

Even so, he could not do much talking. Captain Stevens tried, too, but he did no better. Once he spent most of a day trying to find out something about the country ahead. He built up little mountains of earth and put pebbles on them for rocks and twigs for trees.

79

But the Indians never seemed to get the idea of what he was asking.

So even without being sure just where they were going, they traveled along the river, still keeping to the tracks of the three wagons. If you travel that way sometime in your car along Interstate 80, you will follow close to where Mose passed more than a hundred years ago. Only you must remember that in order to have grass and water the emigrants kept nearer the river than the highway does.

Just the same, the Stevens party moved along very well for a wagon train. There was always plenty of good grass, so the oxen fed well and kept their strength up.

There was no trouble with the Indians— that is, no real trouble. Often, though, the Diggers were a nuisance, for they would come into camp, very friendly but wanting something to eat and peeking into everything. They were likely to pick up anything that was not fastened down and take it away with them. They did not look upon this as stealing.

Yet it was better to put up with them and treat them well. Otherwise they might have become real enemies and have caused much greater trouble.

By now everyone was getting tired of traveling. The novelty had worn off. Though there was a good deal of uncertainty, there was no danger from day to day. There was no game except for a few antelope, and these were not worth the trouble. Besides, the horses were tired now, and it was better to save their strength and not exhaust them by hunts. On all this part of the journey—and it was three hundred miles—Mose had no adventures. Each day was just the same as the day before. As Mose summed it up, "The

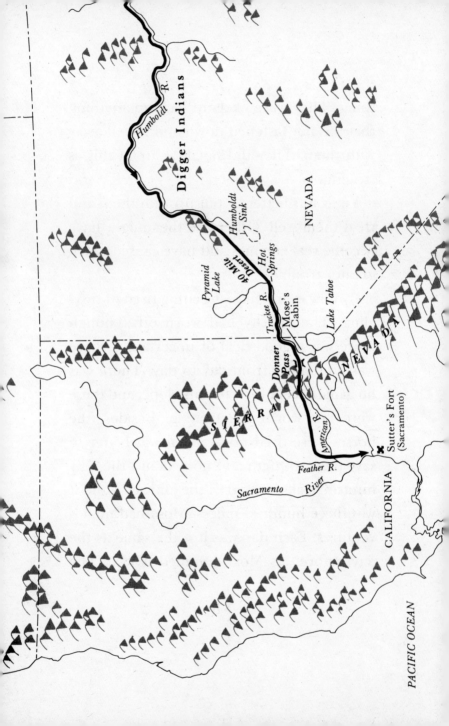

journey down the Humboldt was very mo-
notonous."

At last they must have begun to notice something strange about the river. Most streams, as they knew, got bigger as you fol-lowed them down, but the Humboldt was getting smaller. Nowhere was it very big, and most of its water came from high mountains near its beginning. As the river flowed along, much of this water evaporated in the sun or sank into the sand. The emigrants came from countries like Ireland and states like Missouri where they had never seen anything like this. They must have scratched their heads and said, "This is a strange country!"

But there comes an end to all rivers, and the Humboldt comes to a very curious end. After the emigrants had been following it for more than three weeks, it began to flow directly south. By this time there was not much water left in it. Finally the river came to a big flat swampy place, and here the water just spread out and disappeared. This place was known as the Sink of the Humboldt. The Stevens party went into camp and got ready to stay for a week.

This was about as disagreeable a spot as you can imagine. It was in the midst of a real desert and was likely to be either blazing hot or bitter cold. At the first of October when Mose and the others arrived there, the weather was hot at midday and cold at night. There was no good water near the sink. All the water tasted bitter with alkali, and some of it was even dangerous to drink.

One of the few things that was good about it was the fine hunting. Many antelope came in to drink the water and graze on the grass. There were birds also—sage hens and many ducks and geese and swans that were migrating south alighted on the little ponds of standing water. So some of the men and boys went hunting every day, and everyone enjoyed a change of food and plenty of it.

But if it was in most ways such a bad place, why did they stop here? There were two reasons.

First, the oxen had to have a rest. Even though the water was poor, the grass was good near Humboldt Sink. One of the wisest things the Stevens party had done was to take good care of the oxen. Many parties pressed on too hard and wore their teams out. But, except for being a little tired, the oxen of the Stevens party were in fine shape. A week's rest and good feed would make them as fit as when they first swam across the Missouri.

But there was a second reason why the party halted at the sink—they didn't know which way to go next. At Fort Hall whoever gave them directions probably said, "Follow the river to the sink." But if anyone had then asked, "What after that?" the reply would probably have been, "Well, California lies south and west—somewhere!"

The wagon tracks still led on. From the sink they went southward across the sand of the desert. But either no one knew what had happened to those wagons, or else everyone knew that they had never reached California. So, either way, no one was sure that it was a good idea to follow the tracks.

Now when Captain Stevens or Moses Schallenberger or anybody else looked all around him at Humboldt Sink, he saw the horizon split into six different sections—mountains, a gap, mountains, a gap, mountains, a gap. With a wagon train you do not travel over the tops of mountains. So that leaves the three gaps. One gap was toward the north; one, toward the west; one, toward the south. The wagons had come to the sink through the gap toward the north. So there was no use going back that way. That left the gap toward the south where the wagon tracks went, and the one toward the west. California lay toward the west and south, and so either way might be equally good or bad. By now these people had learned a great deal. They were not going to dash off over an unknown route as they had between Big Sandy and Green River. This was bad country, desert country. A mistake might mean disaster and even death.

When you are lost in a strange country, a good thing to do is to ask directions of someone who lives there. The white people had been very scornful of the poor Diggers, but now they had to go and ask advice. There was a band of them living at the sink, and they were friendly as usual.

8 _____

Truckee

The chief of this band of Indians was an old man. At least he seemed old to Mose. But these desert Indians lived such hard lives, going cold and hungry so often, that they soon came to look old even when they were still young.

The chief's band probably did not number more than fifty people or a hundred at the most. And he was not dressed in fine deerskins, nor did he have a showy head-dress of eagle feathers. No, most of the time he wore nothing but a small apron of skins around his middle, and in cold weather he had a short cape of rabbit fur.

The people of the wagon train called him Truckee. This was not really his name, but they thought it was. When they had first tried to talk with him, he had often answered with a word that sounded like Truckee. Really he was just trying to be agreeable, and the word meant *Very good!* or *Fine!*

Old Greenwood and some of the others went to Truckee and tried to ask him about which way they should be heading. Greenwood used his signs and what words he knew. Truckee was silent. He watched and listened. And after a while he seemed to get the idea. Then he did a remarkable thing.

Truckee squatted down on a smooth spot of ground and Greenwood squatted too, and they began to draw lines on the ground.

After a while they worked out a kind of map. This was all the more amazing for Truckee to be able to do, because he had certainly never seen a book or a real map in his life.

From the map in the sand, the white men thought that they learned a great deal. They should go to the west, not to the south. They would have to travel, they thought, fifty or sixty miles, and then they would come to a river. This river flowed from west to east, not from east to west as the Humboldt did. It flowed out from mountains, and along it were large trees and good grass.

This all sounded fine—in fact, almost too good to be true. This river must flow down from the Sierra Nevada, and just on the other side of that range of mountains lay California.

But could they trust Truckee's map? Perhaps he did not even know what they were asking him. Perhaps he did not really know about the river, and was just pretending, as some people do, because he knew they wanted to find a river. Perhaps he was trying to get rid of them and was luring them into some desert where they would all die of thirst. It would be better to explore.

So three men got ready to set out on horseback. They were Captain Stevens and Dr. Townsend, Mose's brother-in-law, and a man named Foster. They took Truckee with them as a guide and also, we suppose, as a hostage. While he was away and in the power of the white men, the other Indians would not start any trouble. We should feel sorry for Truckee. Probably he had never ridden a horse, and now he either had to go along on foot and keep up with the men on horseback, or else he had to ride a horse and get very stiff.

These four set out toward the west. Mose and the others, from their camp at the sink, must have watched them for a long way. Then when the horsemen disappeared over a faraway rise, the others spent an anxious time waiting. Now that it was October, the weather was getting cold. To try to cross the Sierra Nevada after snow had begun to fall would be very difficult and might be impossible. But the food was getting low. If they tried to pass the winter on this side of the mountains, they might all die of cold and hunger. Still, there was nothing to do but to wait until they found out what lay ahead.

They waited three days. Then the scouts came back. Just by looking at their faces you could have told that everything was fine. They reported that they had found the river, and that it was all as Truckee had described it!

Even yet, of course, no one knew for sure that this was the right way to get to California. But at least this got them across the desert, and no one had any better ideas. They prepared to get going.

On the morning of the start, Mose's temper got him into trouble. Many Indians were hanging about the camp. Mose was saddling his horse, and he found that the halter was missing. He looked around for it and saw an end of it sticking out from under a short cloak worn by an Indian. Mose asked for the halter, but the Indian paid no attention. Mose tried to explain, but the Indian still pretended to know nothing even though the end of the halter was in plain sight. Mose began to get angry. He stepped up and grabbed the end of the halter. The Indian jumped back and drew his bow. Mose ran to the wagon, seized his rifle, and leveled it at the Indian. He was wildly angry and was just about to pull the trigger when another man jumped in and knocked the rifle out of his hand.

Now the whole camp was in confusion— Indians putting arrows to their bowstrings, white men seizing their rifles, women and children running for the shelter of the wagons. It looked as if there would be a real fight.

But the cooler ones like Captain Stevens and Dr. Townsend stepped in to stop the trouble, and probably Truckee was just as anxious on his side to prevent a battle. Things quieted down. The Indian had really been to blame, in the first place, by stealing the halter, but this was no time to stand on the rights and wrongs of a matter. And, after all, no one had asked the white men to come and make their camp right in the middle of the Indians' country.

So the matter was smoothed over. The Indians were given presents to make them feel better, and things got quiet again.

As for Mose, Dr. Townsend talked very severely to him about how foolish he had been to lose his temper and endanger the lives of everybody just because of such a little matter as a horse's halter. He should have known by this time that the Indians were likely to pick up anything that took their fancy. Mose could only say that he was very sorry for having acted like a boy and not like a grown man.

Now came the cry, "Catch up your teams!" and the wagon train got started. Everyone must have been very happy to be leaving the dreary sink of the Humboldt. Also they were leaving the Indian camp behind, and that must have been a relief after what had just happened. But still they must have been worried, too, for now they were setting out into unknown desert country. They were leaving the tracks of the three wagons that they had followed for so long.

The stretch of country that the Stevens party was setting out to cross was a desert about forty miles long.

The Stevens party was in fine shape for the long desert pull. Their oxen were rested and had fed well on the grass at the sink. The women had cooked plenty of food for a two-day journey, and for water the men had filled all the jugs and pots and buckets.

Starting in the early morning, they pushed on all day with scarcely a halt. There were no more wheel marks, and the only trail was that left by the hoofprints of the scouts who had explored ahead. But the country was fairly level, and there was no difficulty in taking the wagons through. The bushes of sagebrush grew two or three feet apart and not much higher than the oxen's knees. So the first wagon could merely crash ahead, the oxen brushing through the bushes, and the wagon wheels crushing them down. The ground was so soft and sandy that the oxen had to pull very hard. The first wagon had the hardest time because its oxen had to break the way. After a while the legs of the lead oxen would become scratched and sore from breaking through the bushes. So the lead wagon would pull aside, and another wagon would go ahead to break trail.

In this way the wagons and people moved on very slowly, making only about a mile an hour. But they kept at it steadily. The sun was behind them in the morning. It rose high at noon and then swung around into the west and shone on their faces. Still they pushed on, hardly stopping at all. The sun set and darkness came, but still they moved ahead. The babies and little children went to sleep in the slowly bumping wagons. The scouts out ahead must have been steering by the stars as one would steer a ship at sea. Or else they were trying to follow the hoofprints through the dark. Now it was midnight, and they came at last to some little hot springs.

Here finally Captain Stevens called a halt. They would stay two hours and rest the oxen.

The poor tired oxen thus had a little time to rest, but nothing else. There was no grass here for them to eat. All the water that could be carried in the wagons was only enough for the people. The springs were boiling hot. Some of the men, pitying their oxen, dipped water out of the springs and poured it into tubs to cool. After a while the oxen could drink it, but this did not work very well either. The water was full of minerals, and the oxen that drank it became sick.

At two o'clock in the morning the still-tired oxen had to settle again to their yokes, and the wagons moved on. After a few hours the country changed again. At daybreak it stretched away level and white without any growth of bushes at all. This was a place where there had once been a lake, but it had dried up hundreds of years before. It had been a salt lake, and now the earth was so filled with salt that nothing could grow there. The ground was soft and dusty, and the oxen sometimes sank in up to their knees. The alkali dust rose all around, and the people sneezed and wheezed with it. Still they pushed on.

Now it was after sunrise and the men began to wonder whether the oxen would ever be able to pull the wagons through. They had not eaten or drunk for more than a day and a half. They were growing weak and were nearly crazy with thirst.

After about five miles of lake bed there came sagebrush country again. By now it was close to noon.

At last the wagons came over a low rise. There, two or three miles ahead, the people saw the fine sight of tall cottonwood trees along the river. When the wagons were still some distance from the water, the oxen began to smell it and became crazier than ever. Then the men wisely halted, and unyoked the oxen from the wagons. The oxen dashed ahead to reach the water. If they had not been unyoked, they might have dashed into the river hauling the wagons behind them and upsetting everything.

After the oxen had drunk and quieted down, they were brought back, and the wagons were hauled to the river. By this time it was well on in the afternoon. The journey across the desert had taken a full day and a full night and nearly all of another day.

The place where the Stevens party came to the river is just about where the little town of Wadsworth, Nevada, now stands. This is the place where Interstate 80 also reaches the river. If you drive through there on a hot day, you too will be very glad to see the fine river and the meadows and the tall green cottonwood trees. You can easily imagine that it must have looked like heaven to Mose and all the other tired people.

It was the best spot that they had seen in many weeks. The water was cold and fresh and clean, not muddy and smelling of alkali. Mose and the other boys must have looked bug-eyed at the big trout lying in the pools. You can guess that some of them ran off to

101

get their fishing lines. And the mothers must have liked the place because there was clean water for washing, and plenty of firewood. There was game, too, and that meant fresh meat—deer in the thickets along the river, and wild ducks and geese and swans flopping down to light on the water.

As far as they knew, this fine river had no name. So, in thanks, they named it for the Indian who had told them of it. And even now it is called Truckee River.

9 _____

At the Pass

This little spot by the river seemed a paradise, but it would not be so when winter came. Already light snows had fallen, making the tops of the mountains white. So after a rest of two days, the people yoked up their oxen and started on again.

The only thing to do now was to try to work up alongside the river as it came down through the mountains. They made good distance for the first few days. Then the mountain sides pressed in closer, and the canyon grew almost V-shaped. In this narrow passageway the river swung back and forth from side to side. Again and again the people had to take their wagons through the water. Once they crossed the river ten times in traveling one mile.

All this meant very slow going and extremely hard work for both men and oxen. The water was cold. The streambed was full of rocks, and often the wagons got stuck. At many crossings the wagons had first to be eased down a steep bank and then hauled up a steep bank at the other side. What was worse—and something no one would have thought of—being in the water so much made the oxen's hoofs grow soft. When the hoofs grew soft, the feet became very tender. The oxen were in such pain they could hardly pull the wagons.

At the same time, the men were being worn

down by all their hard work. Yet they did not dare to stop and rest, for on the mountaintops the glitter of snow gave warning that winter was near.

One day the wagon train came out into a little valley surrounded by mountains where the city of Reno now stands. They had an easy time crossing this.

Still following up the river, they had to enter the canyon again. By now the country had changed, and instead of ugly and bare desert mountains there were mountains covered with pine trees. But otherwise it was even worse than before. Now between the mountainsides and the river, there was often no room even for an ox to walk, much less to pull a wagon. The only thing to do was to haul the wagons right up the river, as if they were boats being taken against the current. The oxen were getting more and more tired, and their feet were growing still softer and more painful. Now the men had to walk beside the oxen all the time in the cold water, or the oxen would simply stop and stand still because of the pain in their feet.

Sometimes the teams for three wagons had to be harnessed to one wagon. Then, with twelve oxen pulling, the one wagon was slowly moved along. After the first wagon had been pulled to a resting place, the teams would have to be taken back twice more to bring up the other two wagons.

No longer was the wagon train making fifteen miles a day, or even ten. Now two miles was a good day's journey.

Then something even worse happened. There came a fall of snow a foot deep. That night the poor, footsore oxen merely stood about and bawled. The snow was so deep that they could not get to the grass that was buried beneath it. Mose tells us that the oxen bawled all night, and the people were so sorry for their poor cattle that they even forgot to be sorry for themselves.

Next day the oxen were not only weary and footsore, but also they were weak with hunger. Still they had to toil on.

For a day or two it looked as if the cattle would starve. The men cut pine boughs, and the cattle ate some of the needles, but this did not seem to help.

Then the wagon train came to a place where some tall rushes grew—too tall to be covered by the snow. The oxen at once began eating these greedily. After that, the scouts located camping spots where there was a growth of these rushes, and so the oxen managed to get along.

The weather was getting colder and colder. More than a month had passed since the

Stevens party had crossed the desert. Now it was nearly the middle of November.

At last they came out from the narrow canyon and crossed a little valley. Only a few miles ahead, a high wall of snow-covered mountains blocked the way. These were the California Mountains, as the emigrants called them. We now use their Spanish name and call them the Sierra Nevada. As far as anybody knows, no white man had ever before crossed these mountains at this point, even on foot or on horseback. Now the Stevens party had to find a way and get across with wagons and with women and children. And winter was at hand.

At a place where the stream forked, they camped and held a council to decide what they should do. Even the boldest and strongest must have been tired and glum.

The first question was, "Which fork of the

stream do we follow?" If they followed the larger one, they would turn to the south. If they followed the smaller one, they would move right against the great jagged wall of mountains. It was much as it had been at Humboldt Sink, and there was no Truckee to draw a map and help them.

They decided to divide. In that way, one group might get through and then be able to send help back to the others.

Four men and two women made ready to follow up the main branch of the stream. They would go on horseback and travel light and fast. They took with them two pack-horses with some provisions, a little extra clothing, and some blankets. The men had rifles and ammunition and hoped to find game. With this party went Mose's friend John Murphy and his sister, Mrs. Townsend. But Dr. Townsend stayed with the main party. All this shows you how bad things were. When families begin splitting up, people are getting desperate.

The main body also agreed to divide. Everyone knew that they could not get all the wagons over these mountains with the oxen in such bad shape. So they left six wagons at the place where the stream forked and made ready to take the other five over the mountains.

The place where this division was made is near where the town of Truckee, California, now stands. The larger stream, flowing from the south, is the Truckee River and is the outlet of Lake Tahoe. The smaller stream, flowing from the west, is Donner Creek.

So the four men and two women on horseback with their two packhorses went off up along the main stream. With them went Mose's sister. He had lived with her ever since he was six years old, and she had been like his mother. Now he might never see her again, for even if one party got through, the other might not.

But he had no time to feel sorry. There was work to be done and plenty of it! Already, we can be sure, Captain Stevens had had the scouts out. Now it was time to yoke up the oxen to the five wagons and be moving.

After a mile or two they came to a long narrow lake. They slowly worked the wagons along the north shore, about four miles, so close that the wagons sometimes seemed to be tipping into the water. Not far beyond the head of the lake they began to ascend the great wall of the pass. To make things worse there was now deep snow on the ground— about two feet of it. The story of what happened then is almost more than we can

111

believe, but we have it as Mose and as others, too, have told it for us.

After they had gone a short way up the pass, the oxen could haul the wagons no farther. Then the men unloaded the wagons and carried all the goods up to the top on their backs through the snow. It must have taken many journeys and have been several days' work.

Then the ox teams were doubled on each of the empty wagons, and the wagons were again hauled farther up, this time about halfway.

At this point there was a cliff like a wall of rock about ten feet high. The men could scramble up, but the oxen could not, much less pull the wagons up over it. It looked as if the wagons might have to be abandoned in spite of everything.

The men searched in both directions and

finally found a small break in this rock wall. It seemed just about wide enough for one ox.

So they unyoked the oxen, and by pushing and hauling, they brought each one up through this little gap.

The oxen were got together again at the top of the rock wall and yoked once more. Then the men linked chains together and let them down over the rock and attached them to a wagon tongue. At the top of the rock wall, the ground was level enough for the oxen to stand and pull. So several teams together pulled on the chains, and at the bottom some of the men lifted up on the wagon wheels. So one by one the wagons were brought up to the top of the cliff.

From there on, the way up to the top was steep and rough and rocky, but it was not as bad as it had been at this one place, and the oxen were able to haul the empty wagons.

Thus the Stevens party became the first ever to get wagons across the Sierra Nevada, and by doing so they opened up the first road to California.

The place where they crossed is known as Donner Pass because of the Donner party who came two years later. It might better be called Stevens Pass. Actually it is only a slightly lower place between high peaks. It is not a broad easy passageway like South Pass by which the emigrants had crossed the Rocky Mountains.

As it happens, this pass is still the main route between San Francisco and the East. The chief railroad and the chief highway cross here. If you come up from Donner Lake and over the pass on Interstate 80, you drive along a fine highway that loops back and forth and in places is blasted out of solid rock. In the summertime you can drive from the lake up to the top of the pass in just a few minutes. But as you go along, look out from the car window and think how hard it would be to bring a wagon up, when there was no road and no time to make one and when two feet of snow covered everything.

As you go along, you can see the remains of various old roads. But these are all later than 1844. To build these various roads so much grading and blasting has been done that now you cannot be certain where the Stevens party came up and just where the wall of rock was. I myself have even climbed up and down that pass many times on foot, and yet I have never been sure. Always I have come back feeling that I did not see how it was done at all, and that it was almost a miracle.

Some of the emigrants themselves thought the same. As one of them tells the story, they were halfway up the mountain, and things looked so bad that even Captain Stevens could think of nothing more to do. Then suddenly he prayed, and after his prayer came a vision showing him the way to go.

Whether we want to think that there was an answer to prayer or whether we want to believe that the emigrants got across by their own skill and courage and hard work, it was a great achievement. The wheels that had crossed from the Missouri River were now ready to roll downhill into California.

10 _____

"Good-bye, Mose!"

In all this great work of crossing the mountains we have lost track of Mose. We last really saw him when he got angry and started to shoot the Indian who had stolen the halter. In the crossing of the desert and the long ascent of the canyon and the final struggle up to the top of the pass, Mose did his work. But nothing special can have happened to him, for he did not bother to tell of it. Now he comes back into the story.

At this time, as you remember, six people

had gone off toward the south on horseback. Most of the others, including all the children, had stayed with the five wagons and were now encamped with them at the top of the pass. Six wagons were still down where the stream forked. These wagons held a large supply of valuable goods, and one of them belonged to Dr. Townsend and Mose. If these wagons were just left there unguarded, the Indians would certainly come after the snow melted and help themselves to everything. So Mose volunteered to stay with these wagons through the winter. Two others said they would stay with him.

One of these was Joseph Foster, one of the three who had ridden across the desert with Truckee. The other was Allen Montgomery, the friend who had been hunting with Mose the time they tried to crawl by the old buffalo bull and had to stay out overnight. Foster and Montgomery were grown men, several years older than Mose.

Mose says that he did not see anything dangerous in staying there along with the two others. They did not have much food, but they were good hunters and thought they could live happily by hunting all winter. The Indians of this region were much like the Diggers and did not seem to be dangerous. Besides, all the Indians would probably move out of the mountains during the winter. As for the snow itself, the three had grown up in the Middle West where there was seldom more than a foot of snow on the ground, except perhaps for a few days after a heavy storm, and so they did not think that there was any chance of being snowed in for long.

The three were probably happy to get away from the work of standing guard over the cattle and yoking up the oxen. Now they

119

could do just as they pleased and go hunting every day if they wanted to. They would build themselves a cabin, and if there came a big snow, they would sit around cozily in the cabin until the snow melted down again. They had seen deer in the woods, and they might even have the luck to shoot a grizzly bear. The party had left two little half-starved cows behind, but the three looked on the cows with scorn. Who would want to eat such tough, scrawny beasts when he could feast on venison and bear meat?

First of all they built a cabin. This too was rather fun. They chopped down small trees, trimmed off the branches, and then used the little cows to haul in the logs. Like all back-woods boys they knew how to notch the ends of the logs and set them up one on another without using any nails.

They laid out a cabin twelve feet wide and

fourteen feet long, a room big enough for the three of them to sleep in and still have a little space left over. They notched the logs carefully so that one fitted tightly on another. But they did not chink in between the logs with mud, probably because mud would have been hard to get with everything under so much snow already. They left a hole for a door, but decided to wait a while before making the door itself. There were no windows, and so the doorway was also for light and air. They built a fireplace of large stones, and above it a big log chimney. On one side of the cabin they built the logs up several feet higher than on the other, and they laid pine branches across for rafters. In the wagons they found some hides, and they laid these hides on top of the rafters for a roof. The little cabin thus had a roof sloping only one way.

All this sounds like a lot of work, but everything was very simply made. With the help of the two cows the whole job took the three of them only two days.

When they had finished the cabin, except for the door, they moved in and felt very snug. They had a big fireplace and plenty of bedding that had been left with the wagons. So they easily kept warm and did not mind the lack of a door.

On the evening of this very day the weather changed, and snow began to fall. In the morning the snow was three feet deep, and the smaller pine trees were bending over with the weight of it. To people who had lived in the Middle West this was a tremendous snowfall, but the three did not worry. They were only annoyed because they had planned to go hunting, and the snow was too deep. Well, the snow would melt, and then they would go hunting. They settled back to wait.

What these three did not realize was that they were actually settling down for a winter in one of the snowiest spots in the world. Here you measure snow by feet, not by inches, and it lasts all winter. The men with the snowplows keep Interstate 80 open, but the snow piles up deeper and deeper until you drive along between snow walls two or three times as high as the car. In spite of the snowplows the road is blocked now and then. Sometimes the snow gets too much even for the trains.

So Mose and the others waited, but the snow did not melt. Instead more snow fell. Day after day it fell. A week passed, and the snow was deeper than ever.

The two poor cows could not find anything to eat, and in fact they could not even move through the deep snow. In pity the men killed the cows to keep them from starving. They were mere skin and bones, and it seemed hardly worthwhile to save the meat. But by now the three were getting just a little worried about this snow; it got deeper and deeper all the time. So they hung the meat on the north side of the cabin and covered it with pine branches to keep any wild animals away. On the north side of the house no sun shone, and so the meat froze and stayed frozen.

Still the snow fell. In two weeks the little cabin was almost snowed under. You could see only the roof sticking out. Mose and the others had to go down into it now through a deep passageway. But actually they hardly ever went outside. The snow was so deep that they could not go anywhere. At most they could keep a path trodden down so that they could get around to the north side of the cabin and cut off more of the tough stringy beef. They were having a hard time getting firewood.

Their faces began to grow thinner and thinner and also longer and longer. Almost their only food supply was the meat of the two starved cows, and this was so tough and stringy that it left a person still hungry. They could not go hunting at all, and even if they could have gone, there was no game. The deer had moved down to the lower slopes of the mountains, and the bears had crawled into caves and hollow logs and gone to sleep for the winter.

This was only about the second week of December, and winter was just beginning. In snow so deep, would anyone be able to come back across the mountains to help them? They began to be afraid that they would starve or freeze there in the deep snow.

They did not even know that any of the others had got through. Perhaps the others were snowed in by this time too. They might even be dead.

By now the three did not go out of the cabin at all except to get some of the little meat that was left or to cut some firewood. They had to flounder around so deeply in the snow that if the firewood had not been close at hand, Mose tells us, they would never have been able to get it.

But these three were not the kind to give up. Sitting there gloomily in their little cabin, they talked of what they might do, and Foster and Montgomery thought of snowshoes. Mose had never seen any or even heard of them. But the other two had either lived in snowier country, or else they had been told of snowshoes, perhaps by Dennis Martin, the Canadian.

It is one thing to think of snowshoes and another thing to make them. But they remembered the long strips of hickory wood that supported the canvas covers of the wagons. Foster and Montgomery took pieces of these and bent them into oval shapes and then filled them in with strips of rawhide. You can imagine with what anxiety they tested out these awkward contraptions.

Yes, they would support a man even on soft snow. He sank in deeply at each step, but that was better than floundering up to his waist or even up to his neck. But it would be taking long chances to try to go all the way over the great mountains on such things, to risk your life on awkward homemade snowshoes.

They hung on a while longer at the cabin, hoping that matters would take a turn for the better. By now there was ten feet of snow!

They went out a little on their snowshoes, taking their rifles along and hoping to see some game. But there was nothing. Sometimes, after there had been a thaw and then a freeze, there was a crust on the snow, and they saw footprints of coyotes and foxes. But they never got a shot.

All three were feeling very blue by this time. They had eaten about half of their meat, and winter had hardly even begun. They would either starve to death or have to try to cross the mountains on their snowshoes. They decided that they would try to cross rather than merely sit and grow weaker day by day.

They dried some of their beef. Each of them took ten pounds of this meat, a pair of blankets, a rifle, and ammunition. Then one morning they left their little cabin and set their faces toward the west.

It was terrible work. They did not really know how to use the clumsy snowshoes. Instead of fastening the snowshoes merely to the toes of their shoes, they fastened them toe and heel. So they had to lift the whole weight of the shoe every time they took a step. To make things worse, the shoes sank deep, and snow fell in from the sides. Soon there was a load of snow on each shoe, so that before long each shoe was carrying a ten-pound weight. They could stop and clean the snow off, but the same thing would soon happen again.

As they went along, Mose found himself falling behind the others. They were grown men, and he was still a boy. It was terrifying for him to see them leaving him behind, and it was bad for them to have to lose minutes by waiting for him to catch up. After a long time—probably it took them all morning—

they got to the head of the lake. Then began the even harder work of climbing up the pass. It was terrible in the deep snow with the heavy, awkward snowshoes. Mose kept falling behind.

About the middle of the afternoon Mose began to have cramps in his legs. The strange way of walking by lifting his foot high at every step was getting to be too much for him. When the cramps hit him, he had to stop and grit his teeth with the pain and wait until it was over. The others could only look down at him from higher up and wait too.

They must have been well up the slope of the pass, and they could see back, miles and miles, toward the east. But it was all lonely mountains, deep in snow. Not a single column of smoke rose anywhere, and there was no one to call on for help.

Mose struggled ahead. Now when the

cramps hit, the pain was so bad that he fell right over into the snow. He could go only about fifty yards and then had to stop and rest. He had to use all his nerve to keep going. But if he stopped, he would just die there. The others could not carry him through the deep snow. About sunset they reached the top of the pass with Mose hardly able to drag himself into camp.

The other two cut down a tree and laid the logs side by side on the snow. On top of this platform of green logs they built a fire of dry wood from a dead tree. They spread some pine branches around on the snow for their beds.

Then they ate a little of their dried meat and stood around the fire trying to keep warm. It was very cold there, after sunset, on top of the pass. Two blankets are not worth much in such a cold. They lay down and

131

tried to sleep, taking turns at getting up and throwing more wood on the fire.

But they could not sleep. They kept thinking that they would probably die and that all the others might have died already. Besides, though the fire kept their feet from freezing, still they were shivering and too cold to sleep.

The next morning the fire was burning at the bottom of a big hole in the snow, having melted its way down during the night. This hole was about fifteen feet deep, and had such steep sides that they could not even get down to where the fire was. This did not matter much because they had nothing to cook anyway.

Foster and Montgomery were still in fairly good shape, but Mose was so stiff that he could hardly move. After he had got to his feet, the three stood at the edge of the deep hole in the snow and chewed a little dried beef for breakfast. They all realized that Mose could not go on across the mountains. If he gave out, the others would either have to leave him behind, or else they would have to stay with him and perhaps lose their own lives, though they could be of no help. So Mose said that he would go back to the cabin by himself. There was still a little beef left there. He would live on that as long as he could, and then he would start across the mountains again by himself.

Mose must have known that he would probably grow weaker at the cabin and might never be able to start across the mountains again. The others must have known it too. But there was nothing better to do. If he stayed with the others, he would merely hinder them and thus cause them also to lose their lives. They were his good friends and his comrades of the long journey, and they did not like to agree to the plan. They may have thought that he would never even be able to get back to the cabin. Perhaps Mose thought so too. They promised that they would send help back to him if they got through to California.

There was not much to say. When everyone was ready to start, Mose shook hands with each of the others. About the only word he spoke was "Good-bye!" And they said, "Good-bye, Mose!"

Then Foster and Montgomery turned and went on through the snow westward. Mose, all by himself, watched them go, and felt a great wave of loneliness come over him.

134

11 _____

Foxes
and Coyotes

That was a low point—when the others left
him. After they had got out of sight and he
was all by himself, Mose began, strangely, to
feel a little more cheerful. At least it was a
relief not to have to keep up with the others.
He began to hope that things might change
for the better. So he strapped his blankets
and dried meat on, shouldered his rifle, put
his snowshoes on, and began to move back to
the cabin. Right away he found that things
really were a little better.

Now he was traveling downhill, and that made it easier. Besides, he followed the trail that the three of them had broken through on the day before, and so the snow was somewhat packed down. Also it had frozen hard during the night. He found that he could walk without the heavy snowshoes. That made all the difference in the world.

Still he had a bad time. He was weak with all that he had gone through on the day before, and at times he thought he would never make it to the cabin.

He got there just before dark and stumbled through the deep passageway between the walls of snow. The log at the bottom of the doorway was only nine inches high, but he was so tired that he could not even raise a foot over it. He had to use his hands to lift each foot across into the cabin.

In the darkness everything seemed gloomy

again, and Mose spent a bad night. He scarcely slept because he was in such pain as well as worried. In the morning he could hardly do more than crawl about the cabin at first. Later he forced himself to put the snowshoes on. He must do something to get food. Taking his rifle, he went out and floundered through the snow, hoping to get a shot at a fox. But Mose knew he had little chance. Foxes are out at night, not in the daytime. He saw tracks but no fox.

Toward evening he came in, tired and very sick at heart. As he was standing his rifle up in the corner of the cabin, he saw something that gave him a sudden idea. In that corner were some steel traps that Captain Stevens had left behind in his wagon. "Ah," thought Mose, "if I can't shoot a coyote or fox, why not trap one?" At once he began to feel better.

Hurrying, before it got dark, he set out to make the traps ready. What should he use for bait? He thought of the heads of the two cows, not much use for eating. He cut them up and baited the traps with them. Then he went about on his snowshoes, finding sheltered places beside fallen trees where he could place the traps. That night he went to bed with a lighter heart and got some sleep.

At daylight he hurried out to look at the traps. He was anxious to see them and yet he dreaded to look for fear he had caught nothing. But in one of them he found a coyote.

The coyote seemed to have been half-starved before it came to the trap. But Mose was in no condition to be choosy. In no time at all he had some of the coyote meat roasting in a Dutch oven.

When the meat was done, he took it out and sat down, eager to eat. He took a bite, and then his face changed. It was horrible! Hungry as he was, he had to force himself to eat.

He thought that he might not have cooked it the right way. How about boiling it? That should make it more tender.

He tried boiling. The coyote was just as bad that way. Then he tried every way of cooking that he could think of, but there was no way of making that meat fit to eat. Yet for three days Mose saved his little store of beef and lived on the coyote.

He had been setting his traps, but for two nights he had caught nothing. Then on the third night he caught two foxes.

Here at least was a change. The foxes did not seem to be so starved as the coyote had been, even though they too were skinny.

Mose roasted one fox, sat down to try it, and had a marvelous surprise. The roast fox was delicious. It was very thin, and he could easily have eaten it all at two meals, but he made one fox last him for two days.

Being a little stronger now, he put on his snowshoes every day and wandered about with his rifle, still hoping to see a deer. But the only living thing he saw was a crow. By good luck he managed to shoot the crow, and he prepared it for eating, thinking that he might like a change. He stewed it, but it turned out to be as bad as the coyote. So Mose kept on eating fox.

Every night he saw that his traps were baited and set. He caught a fox about once in every two days, and this just kept him going. Every now and then also he caught a coyote. He lived on the foxes and kept the coyotes as a reserve, hanging them up on the north side of the cabin where they froze. In this way he went on from day to day, having enough to eat, but always being afraid that he would use up the supply of foxes in the neighborhood and have to eat coyote again or even face starvation.

One day, as Mose approached one of his traps, he saw a fox caught in it. As Mose came nearer, the fox managed to escape from the trap and limped away, badly crippled. The thought of losing even a single fox was more than Mose could bear. He hurried back to the cabin as fast as he could and got his rifle. Then he followed the trail of the fox. In the meantime the fox had gone across to the other side of the creek. Mose managed to get a shot, and then the problem was how to get to where the fox was lying. The creek was two and a half feet deep and icy cold.

Mose had to take off his snowshoes. Then he waded into the icy water and across on the other side he had to wallow forty yards through the deep snow, sinking clear to his armpits. Finally he reached the fox and returned. All this shows how desperately Mose strove for food—risking death from freezing and from pneumonia just to get a single fox.

Yet from day to day he got enough to eat. He had no bread of any kind, but the meat seemed to be all he needed. He did not even use salt on it, although he had plenty.

He had enough coffee for just one cup, and for a while he saved this too. Then, one day, having kept track of time, he knew that it was December 25. So he made himself a cup of coffee to celebrate Christmas.

Day after day and week after week! He was absolutely alone in the deep snow, surrounded by high mountains. He worried a good deal about himself, and also about the others—his sister and Dr. Townsend and all his friends.

He kept track of the days. Now it was well into January. At noon now, the sun was just a little higher in the sky, but still the snow fell. When he went outdoors he could hardly see the cabin at all because of the snow. Would spring never come?

Often he lay awake in the night, wondering what he would do if there were no more foxes—or not even coyotes. He decided that then he would take what was left of the beef and again try to get over the pass on the snowshoes. But always there was another fox in one of the traps. He was afraid to eat as much as he wanted, and so he was always a little hungry, but he was never really starving.

And the line of coyotes hanging up on the north side of the cabin got longer. First there had been just one, and then there were two and then three. After a while there were five, and then there were seven. Mose never could bring himself around to trying coyote again. If he had, he might have been surprised. For that first time he had probably happened to get an unusually tough old coyote. A young coyote might have tasted quite as good as a fox.

Besides worrying about having enough to eat, the worst thing was to find something to do. Here he had a bit of luck. In Dr. Townsend's wagon he found some books. So he read a great deal. Even after dark he always built a large fire and put pine knots on it. When pine knots burn, they send out a bright light. So Mose was able to read late into the nights, and then he could sleep later the next morning and the day seemed shorter.

We would like to know what books Mose read, but he has not told much. Probably there was a Bible, and if he read in it, we would hope that he came to the part where Elijah lives by himself beside the brook and the ravens bring him food, day by day. We would wish also that he could have had *Robinson Crusoe*, for in many ways Mose was living in his cabin much as Crusoe lived on his island all alone. But we know the names of only two of his books. He read the letters that Lord Chesterfield wrote to his son, telling him how to behave in polite society. This seems a strange book for Mose to have been reading when he had no society at all. And he also read Byron's poems. This was perhaps a better book, for there are many fine descriptions of storms and mountains.

In spite of his books, the days were long. Still, they passed, and Mose checked them off one by one. Now it was the first day of February.

Something that got to bother him more and more was the silence. During the storms he heard the wind blowing through the trees. Sometimes, when the snow was falling quietly, there would come a long *sh-sh-sh* as it slid off a tree. But that was all. There was no sound of man or beast or bird. In the clear cold nights the stars glittered overhead, seeming close above the mountain peaks— but there was no sound. Just to break the fearful silence, Mose sometimes read aloud from his books, and sometimes he even talked to himself.

Still he checked off the days slowly. He watched the sun get higher and warmer. Would the snow never melt? Now it was getting well along in February. Mose had been alone by himself for nearly three months. It seemed years. Yet he was getting along. There were still foxes, and he had his little reserve of beef. The line of coyotes was longer. Now there were eleven.

One evening, a little before sunset, on a day that was close to the end of February, Mose was standing near the cabin. He looked toward the pass, and suddenly his heart almost stopped beating. Far off, through the trees, he saw something moving. It might be a man.

He scarcely dared to look. Yes, it was a man! But it might be an Indian.

No, it did not look like an Indian. The man was on snowshoes and moving quickly across the snow. Then new hope flooded in upon Mose. He was saved! He knew that man! It was his old comrade, the Canadian, Dennis Martin!

12 _____

End of
the Trail

There isn't much more to tell of Moses
Schallenberger and how the first wagons
came across to California.

Dennis Martin, being a Canadian, knew a
great deal about snowshoes and how to use
them. So it was he who had come across the
mountains all by himself, risking his own life,
to see whether Mose was still alive and to
help him out.

Martin made better snowshoes for Mose
and showed him how to use them. On the

148

very next morning the two of them set out to cross the pass. Mose had a hard struggle, but this time he made it.

From Martin, Mose must have heard the news, and it was all good news. Everybody was safe—even Foster and Montgomery!

The six who had gone on horseback, including Mose's sister, had had a hard time, and John Murphy had almost drowned when trying to swim his horse across the swift-running American River. But they had all got through. They told of coming to a beautiful lake in the mountains, and so we know that they were the first white people ever to stand on the shore of Lake Tahoe.

Those who went across with the wagons had been snowbound for a while, but they too were all safe. In fact, this party was larger than when it had crossed the pass, for in one of their camps a baby was born to Mrs. Martin Murphy.

The baby was a girl, and they called her Elizabeth. As you remember, there had already been a baby born at Independence Rock. So when the Stevens party finally got through to California, there were two more of them than there were to begin with.

Also, they still had most of their oxen and horses, and the next summer some of the men went back with ox teams to get the six wagons that Mose had watched all winter. Unfortunately, after the snow had melted, the Indians had found the wagons and had taken everything out of them except the guns and ammunition, which they were afraid of. But the wagons themselves were worth good money, and the men harnessed up the oxen and brought the wagons across. So the only loss was the goods in those six wagons.

You may be ready to say, "How lucky they

were!" But it was not all luck. The people in the Stevens party got through so well because they used their heads. They did not quarrel among themselves. They did not get panicky and do foolish things. They kept on good terms with the Indians. They took care of their oxen. In Captain Stevens, they had a fine leader.

You will want to know what happened to Mose after he got to California. Well, first he lived in the town of Monterey and was a clerk in a store. When gold was discovered, he went to the mines with five cartloads of goods. He sold these at high prices for gold dust and made money. A few years later he settled on a farm in San Jose, near San Francisco Bay. He did well and soon married. He and his wife had five children. Mose—or I suppose we should now say Mr. Schallenberger— grew a long beard and lived to be over eighty.

So apparently it does a boy no harm to live on foxes for a while.

As he got older, he thought more about his early days and wrote down the story of the journey. Also, as a souvenir he always kept a wheel from one of the wagons.

Mose—or Mr. Schallenberger—was right to be proud of that journey. What those people did was heroic, and it was also important in history. They took the first covered wagons to California. In the next year a few more wagons crossed, following the same trail, and in the three years after that came a great many wagons. Then 1849 was the year of the gold rush. By this time there were also some other trails that later wagon trains had opened up. But still, Mose and his companions were the ones who showed it could be done.